COOPER'S HAWKS

Studies for Wildlife Artists

Photography and Text

by

Al Lodwick

First Edition 2015

ISBN 978-1516909865

DEDICATION

To Ann Lodwick, my wife and best friend for nearly thirty-eight years.

ACKNOWLEDGEMENTS

Scott Mies for encouragement and editorial advice.

Rachel Lodwick for the Mieswick, LLC logo.

Victoria Tubbs for the author's photograph.

INTRODUCTION

This book is the result of five years of nature photography in the biologically diverse central highlands of Arizona around Prescott. The Arizona highlands are not what most people imagine when they first think of Arizona. At the lowest level you find desert grassland. This gives way to Oak-Pinyon-Juniper woodland. Higher still are the tall Ponderosa Pines – a stand of trees stretching hundreds of miles in Arizona and New Mexico. At the highest levels you find Douglas Fir forest. Throughout the highlands you find an intermingling of both flora and fauna from both hotter and colder climates. For example, you can find hedgehog cacti growing at the roots of Ponderosa Pines.

Nesting in the tall Ponderosa Pines you may be fortunate enough to see Cooper's Hawks. These birds are called accipiters because they prey on other birds. They will use the Ponderosas and almost any other tree to perch and conceal themselves for ambush attacks.

The emphasis of this book is to depict scenes for wildlife artists that are not easily seen with the unaided eye. Examples of this are the different eye colors and plumage patterns in juveniles and adults, how the bill and tongue look when the birds are calling, how they hold their prey when eating, and how the wings bend on takeoff. This book will be of great assistance in getting every detail "just right".

The author hopes that non-artists will also enjoy the pictures and learn more about these magnificent birds and the habitats of the highlands of central Arizona.

Al Lodwick
Prescott, Arizona
August 2015

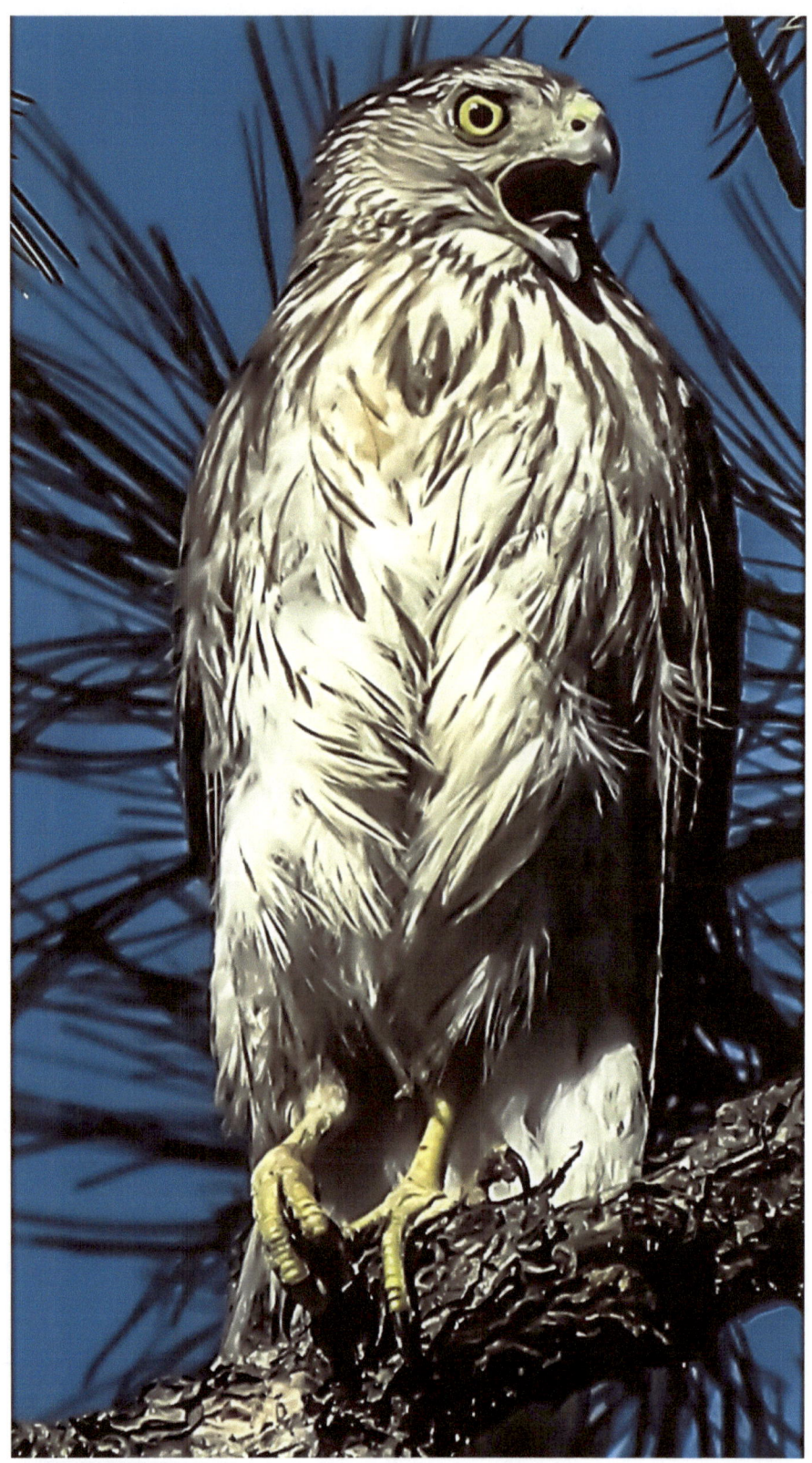

Cooper's Hawks weigh between one-half and about one pound. The females tend to be larger than the males. Those living east of the Mississippi River tend to be larger than those in the west. Note its tongue when calling.

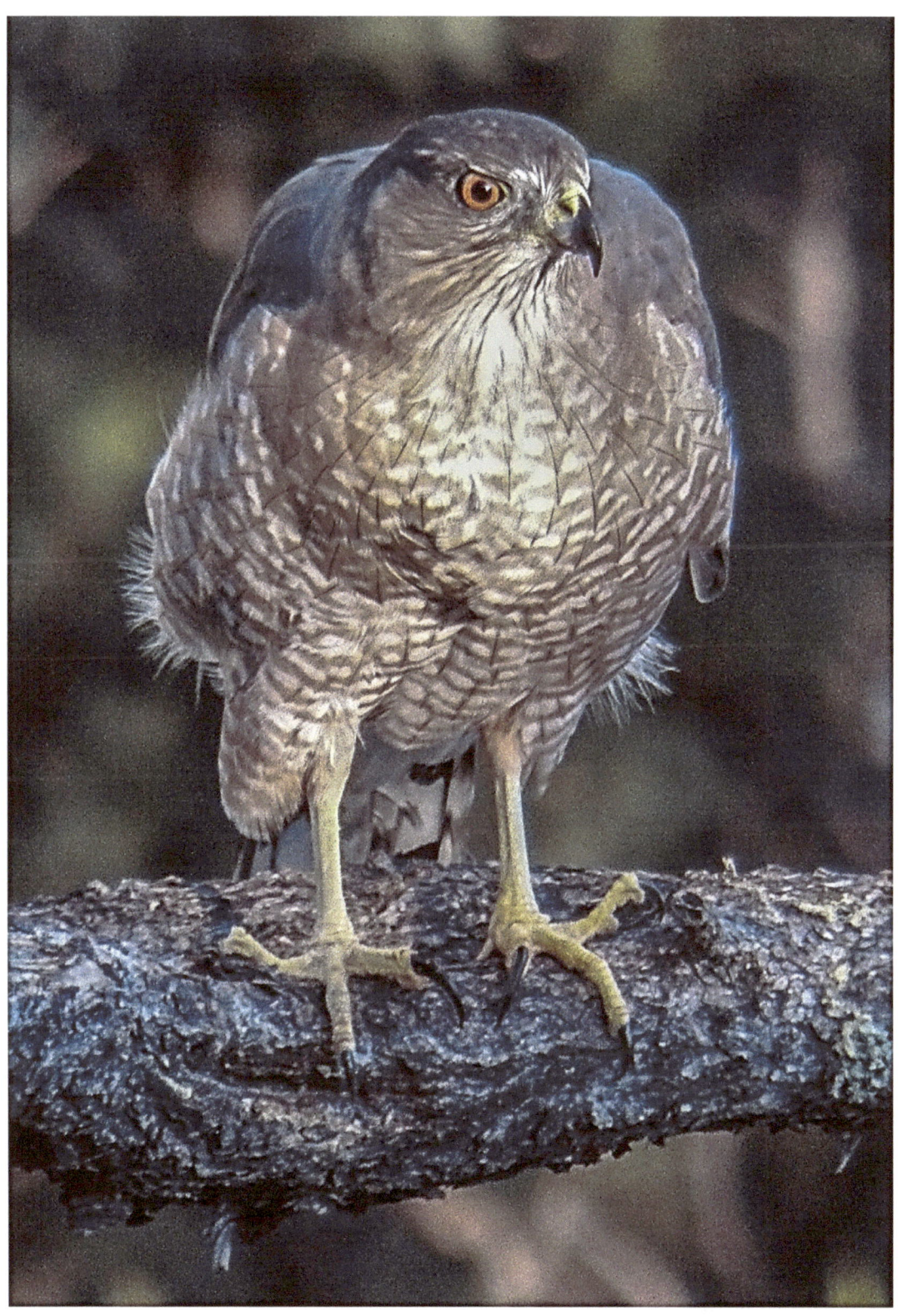

One of the main distinguishing features between adults and juveniles is eye color. Mature Cooper's Hawks have red eyes while juveniles are yellow. Compare this adult bird with the juvenile on the previous page.

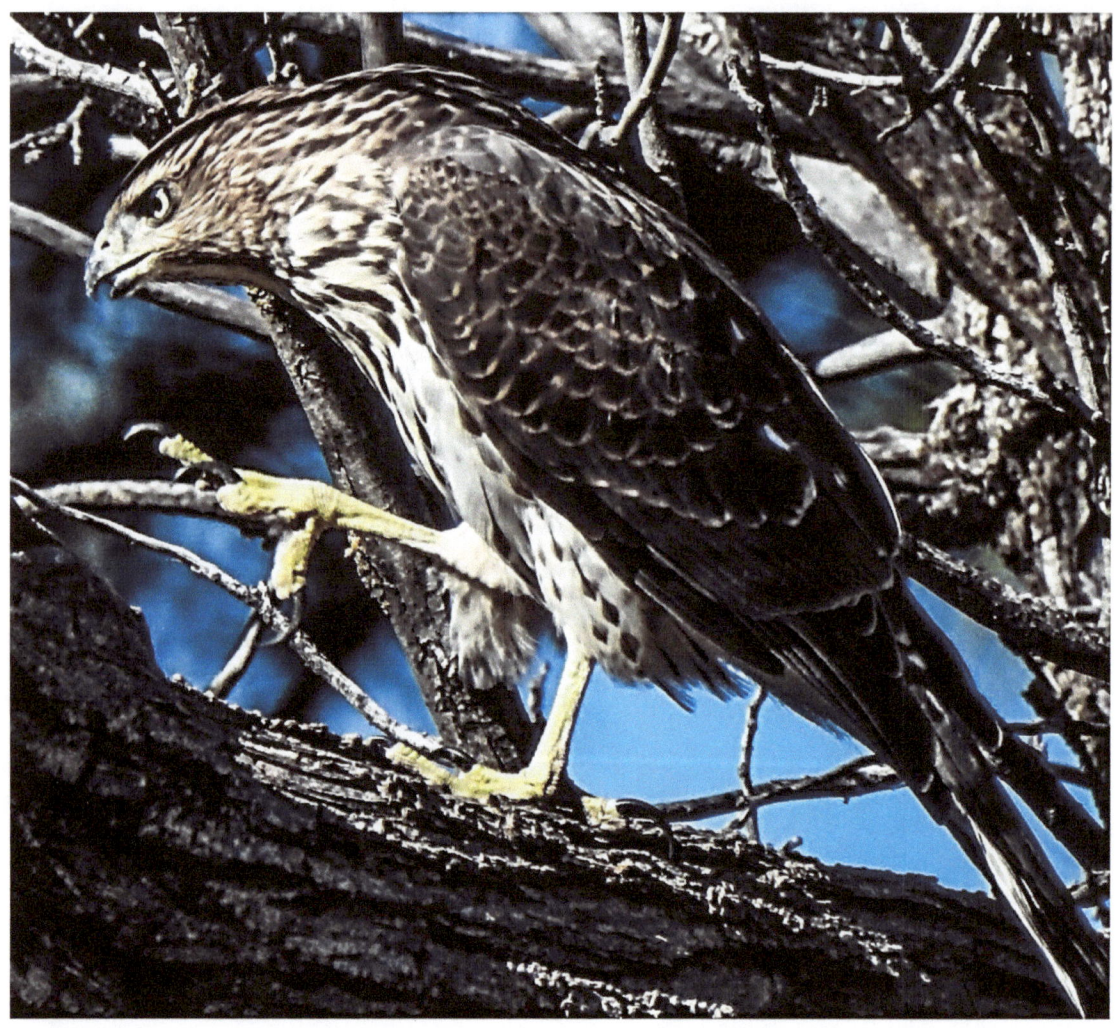

Cooper's Hawks are accipiters. That means that their primary prey is other birds. They mainly pluck other birds out of the air while both are in flight. If its prey chooses to sit under cover the hawk will stalk it as this one seems to be doing

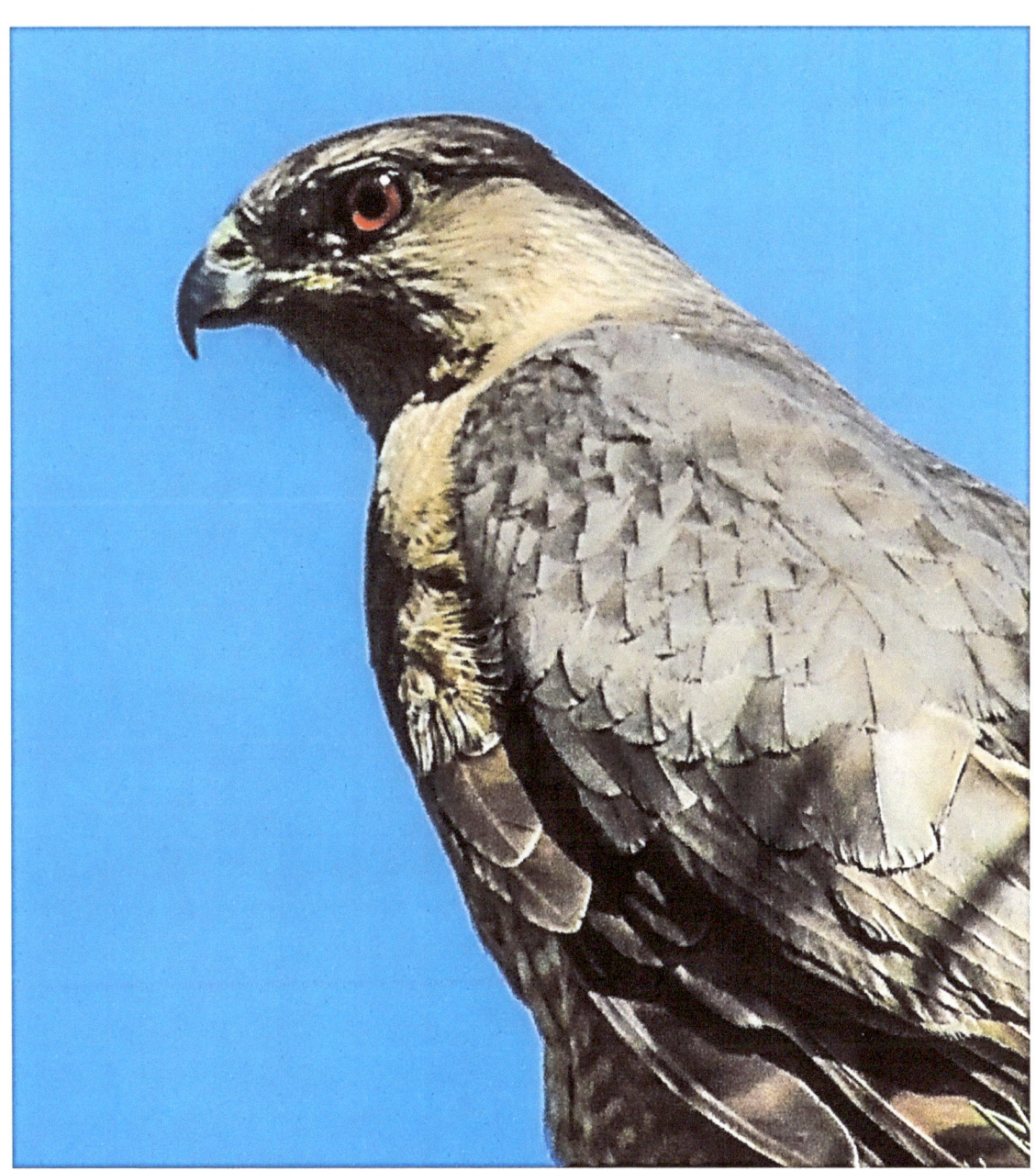

The hooked portion of the bill is called the cere. It is a hallmark of a bird of prey. The cere is very efficient in ripping the flesh of prey that has been crushed in the hawk's strong talons. Note again the different plumages between the juvenile of the previous page and the adult on this page.

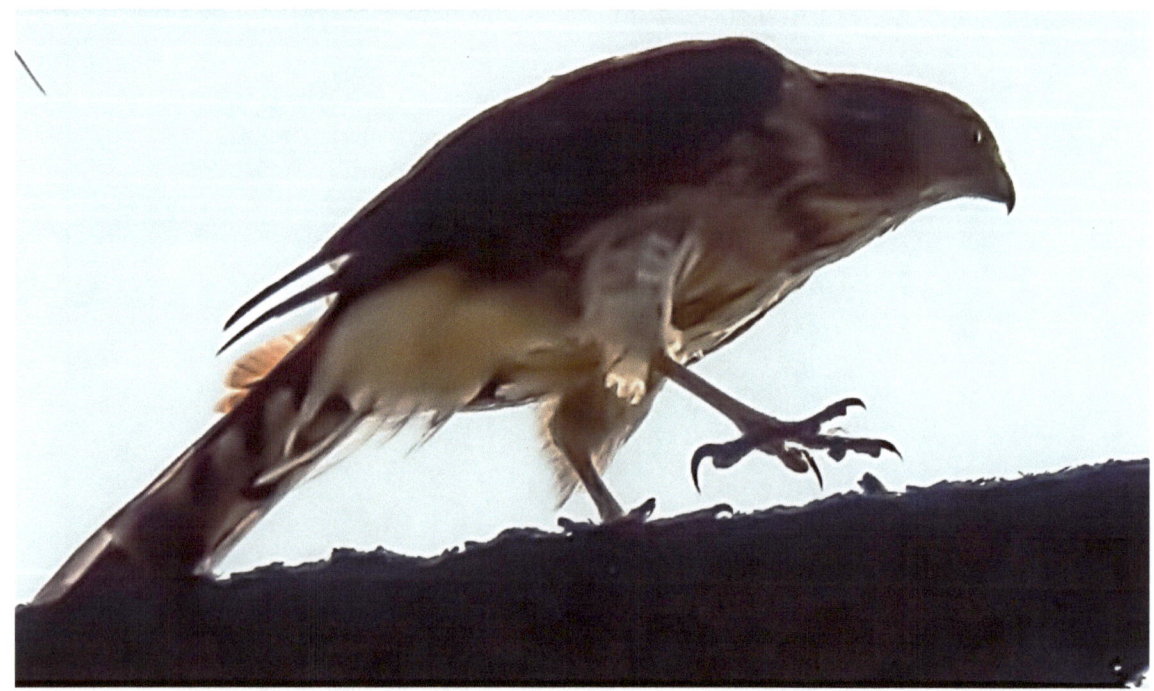

Talons are another requirement for being a bird of prey. A Cooper's Hawk always catches its prey with its talons and then crushes it to death. While the prey is dying, they hold it away from their bodies so that they are less vulnerable to any counter-attack.

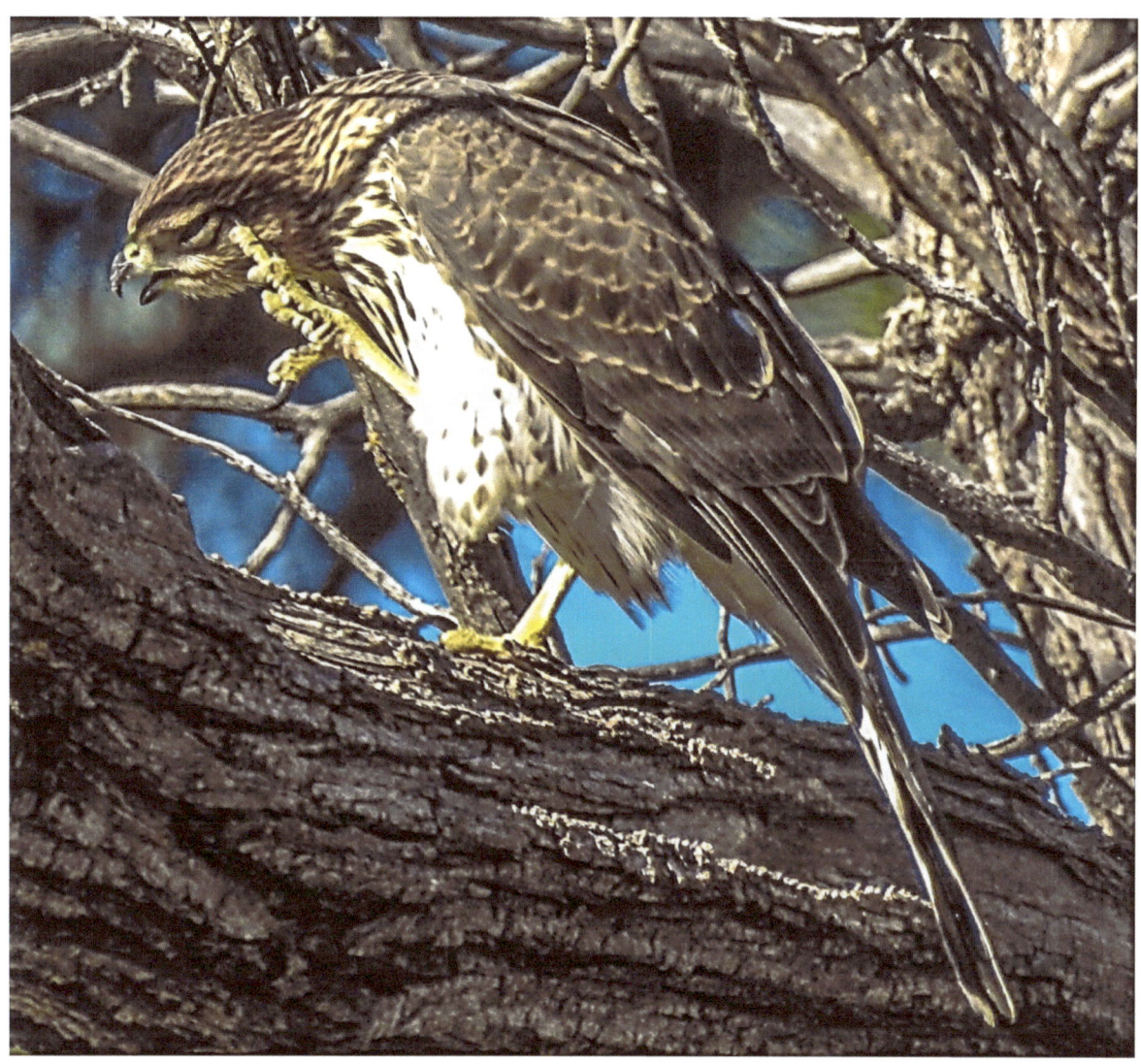

Cooper's Hawks can be quite tolerant of people. This one landed quite close to me because it needed to scratch. Note the look of relief on its face. Even the mighty can be brought down by parasites.

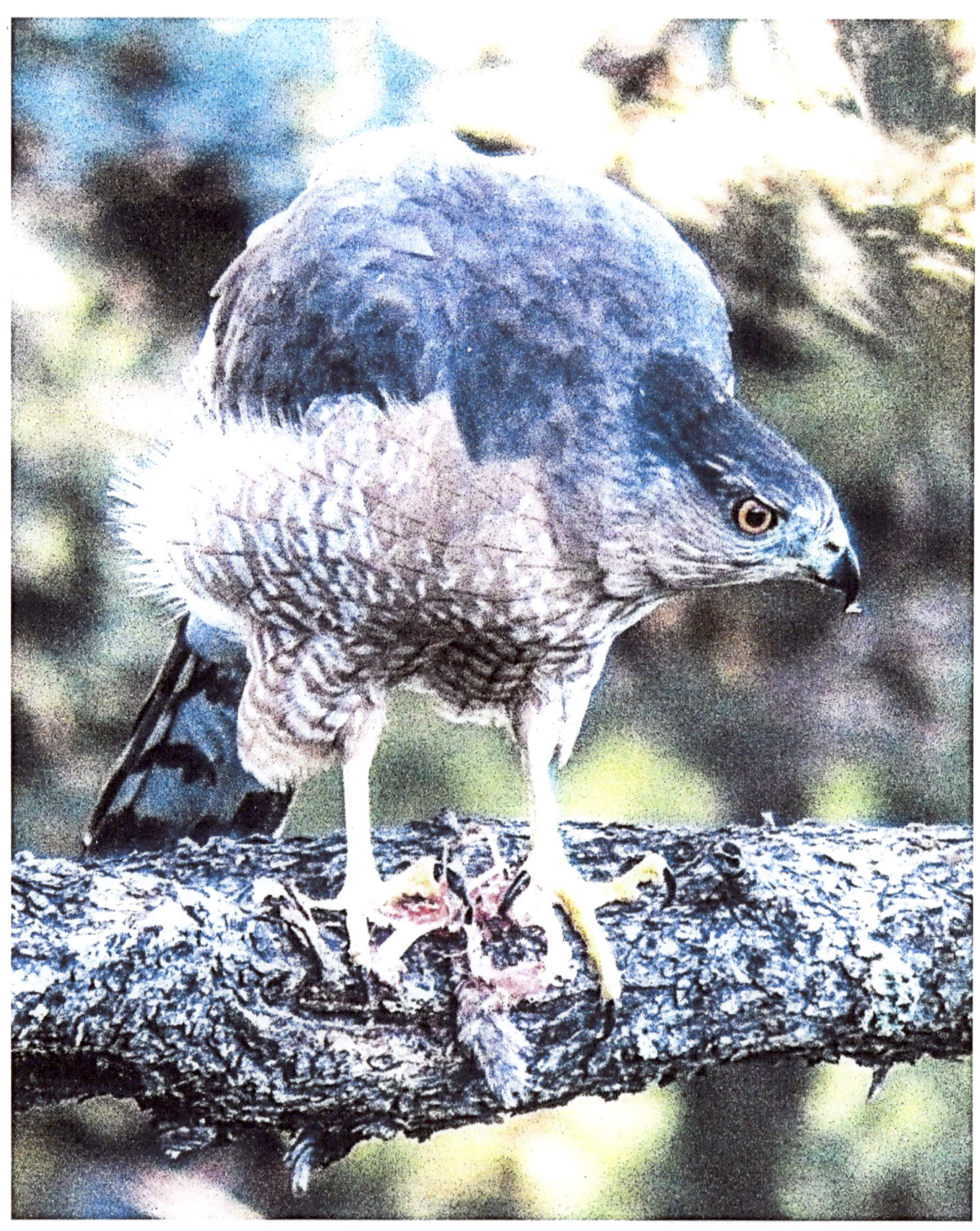

The next several pages will feature a mature Cooper's Hawk consuming a catch. If you choose to not show the bloody portions you can still use these pictures to show various postures typical of these birds.

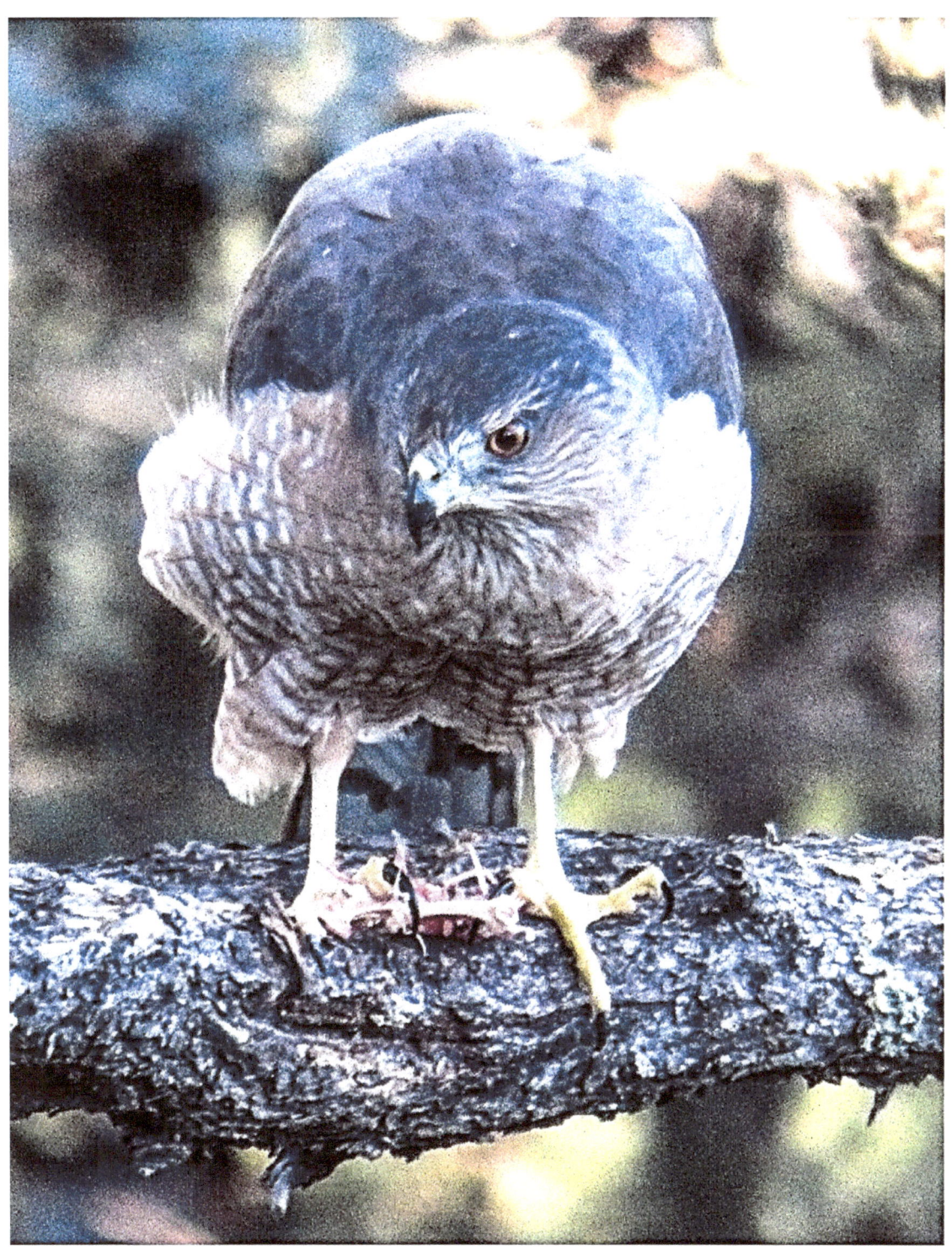

Cooper's Hawks will go after almost any bird that is smaller than it is. From the size of the thigh bone between its talons the prey must have been fairly large; perhaps a Gambel's Quail.

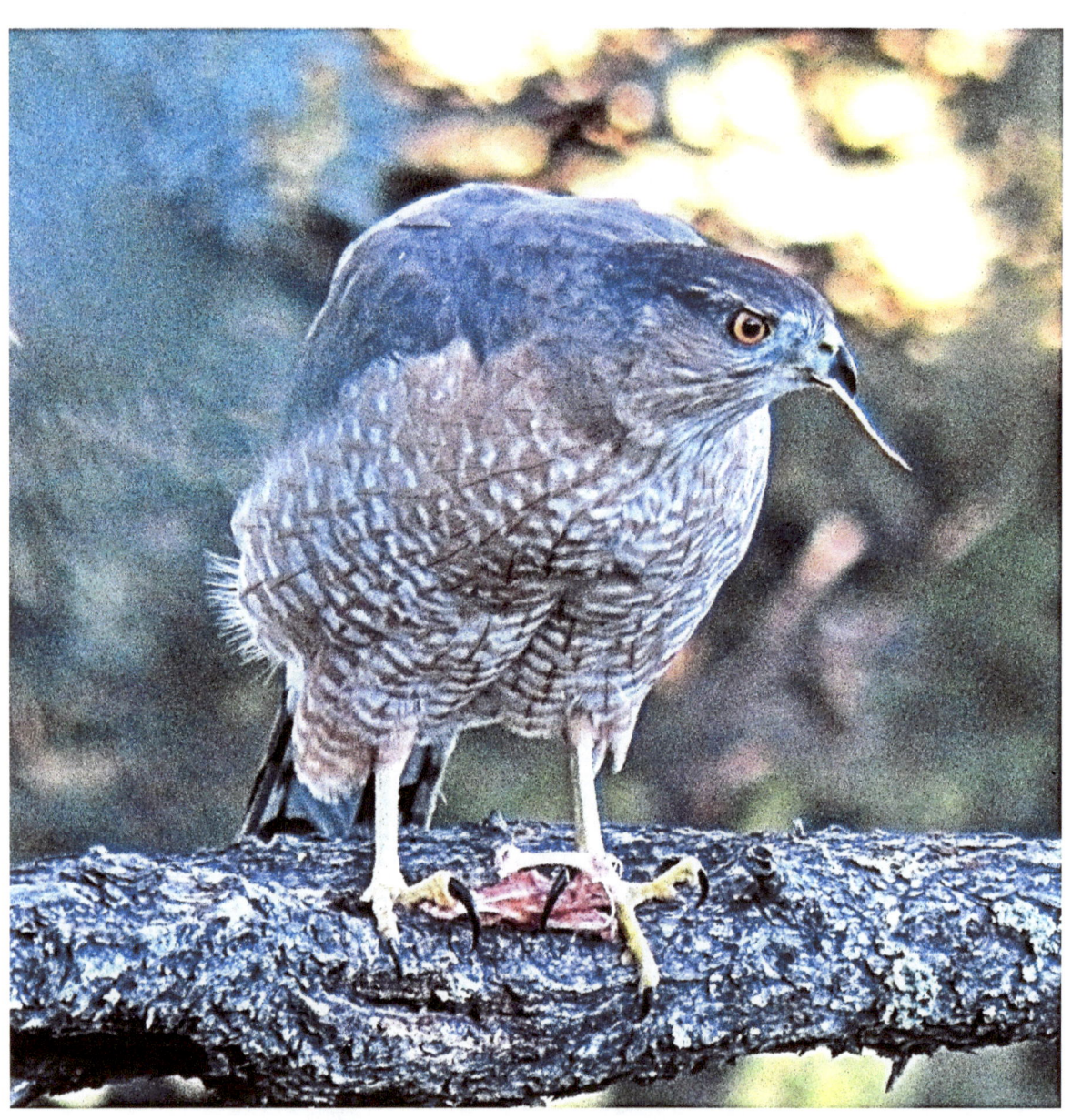

This picture illustrates how the cere of a Cooper's Hawk is well suited for ripping flesh. It appears to be a tendon that is in this bird's bill.

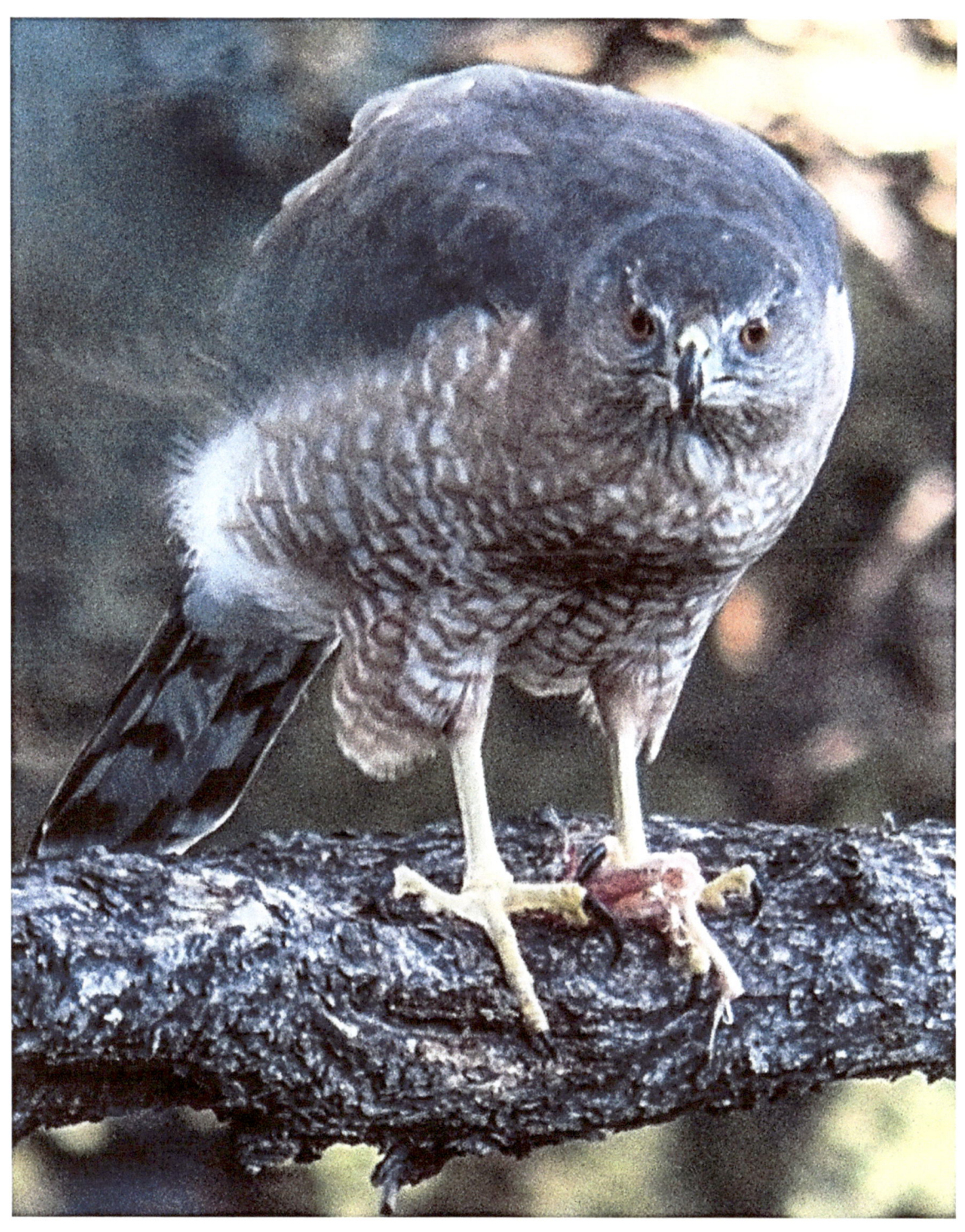

Even though a Cooper's Hawk is near the apex of the food chain it must constantly be vigilant for other predators and scavengers that could be threats.

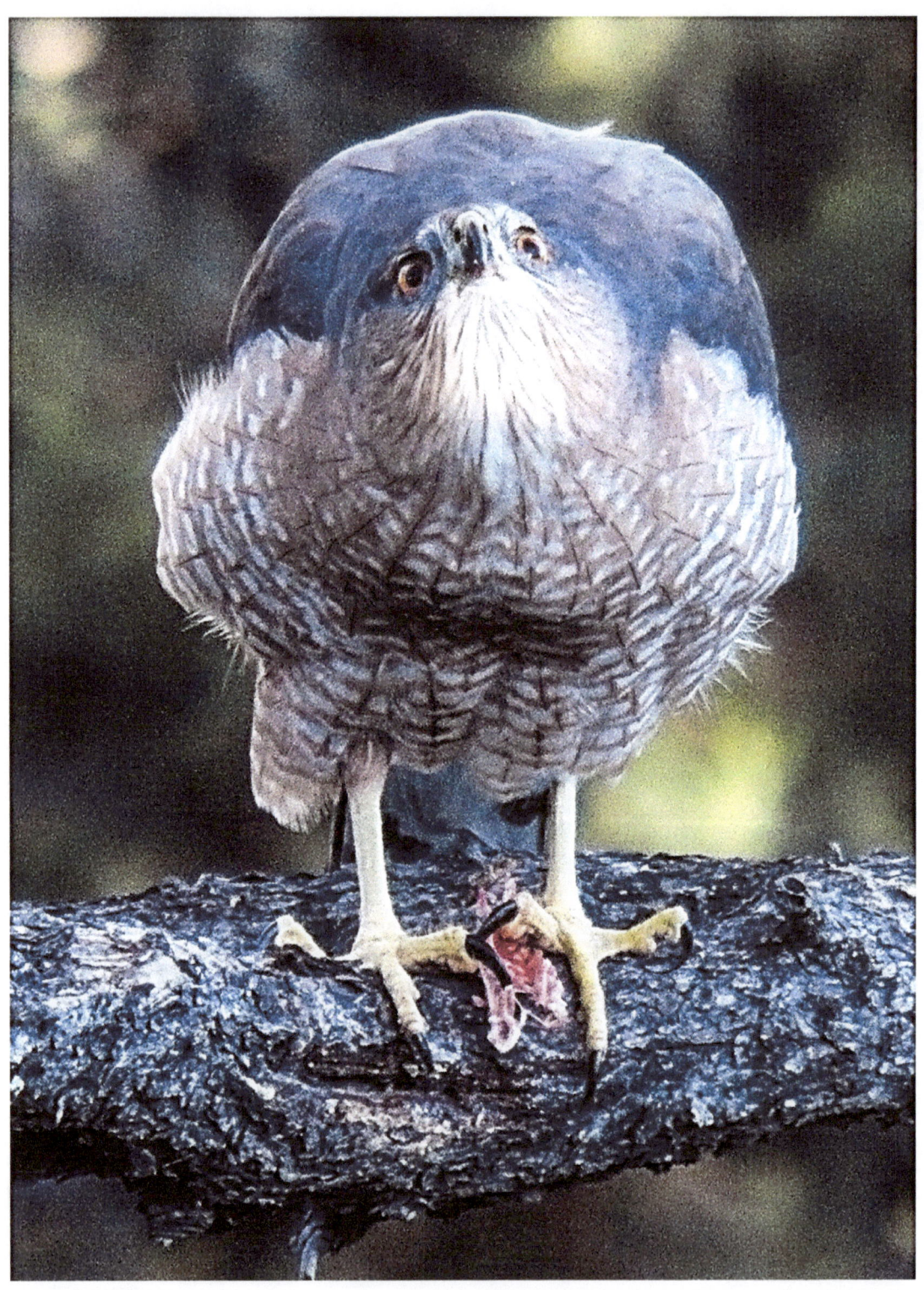

A Bald Eagle flying overhead is a cause for concern for a Cooper's Hawk. Bald Eagles generally do not prey on hawks, but one can never be too careful. Note how the eyes of a predator look forward providing 3-dimensional vision; essential for quickly capturing prey.

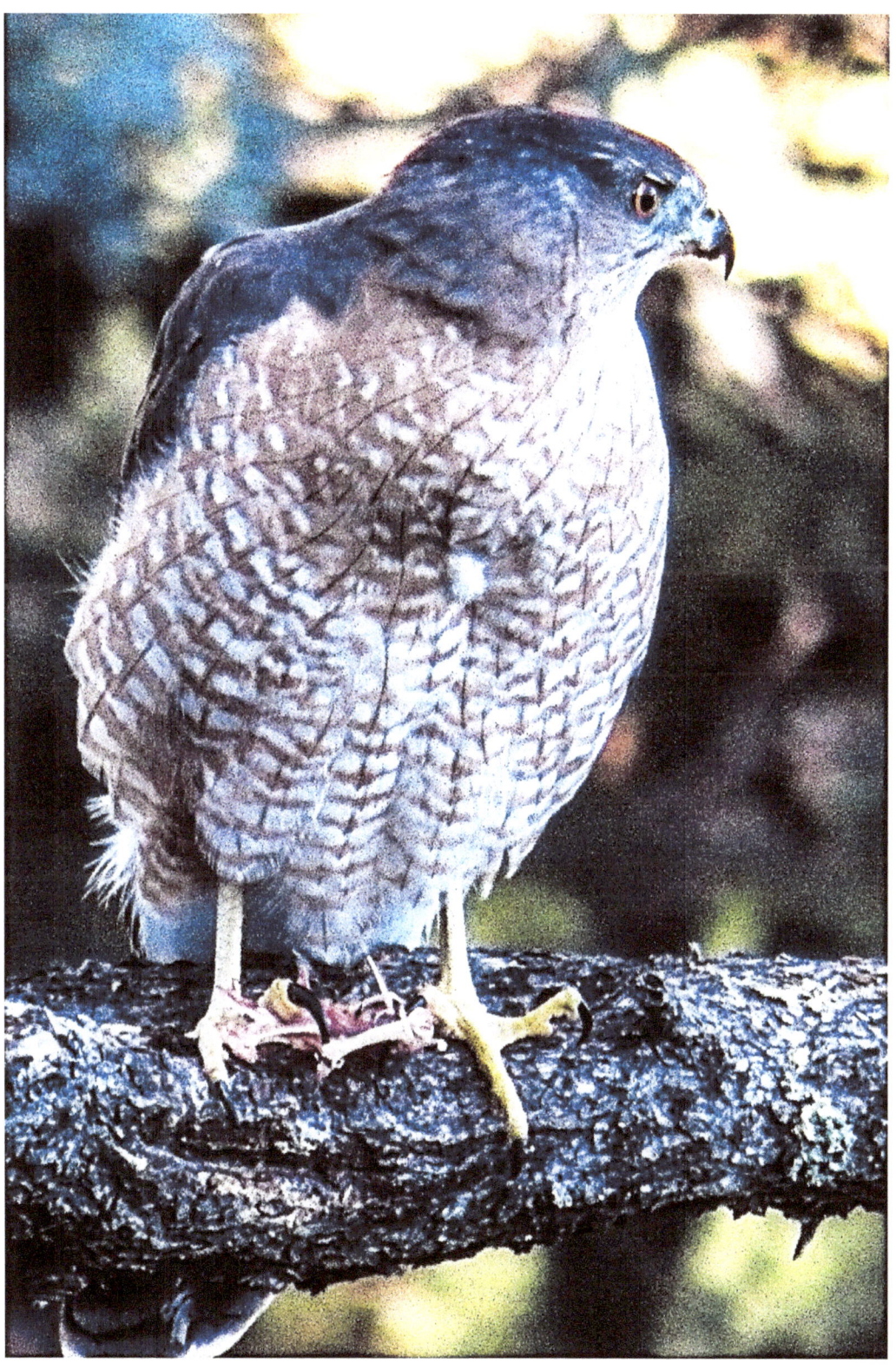

In this picture notice the size and shape of the cere and how the eyes are oriented toward looking forward.

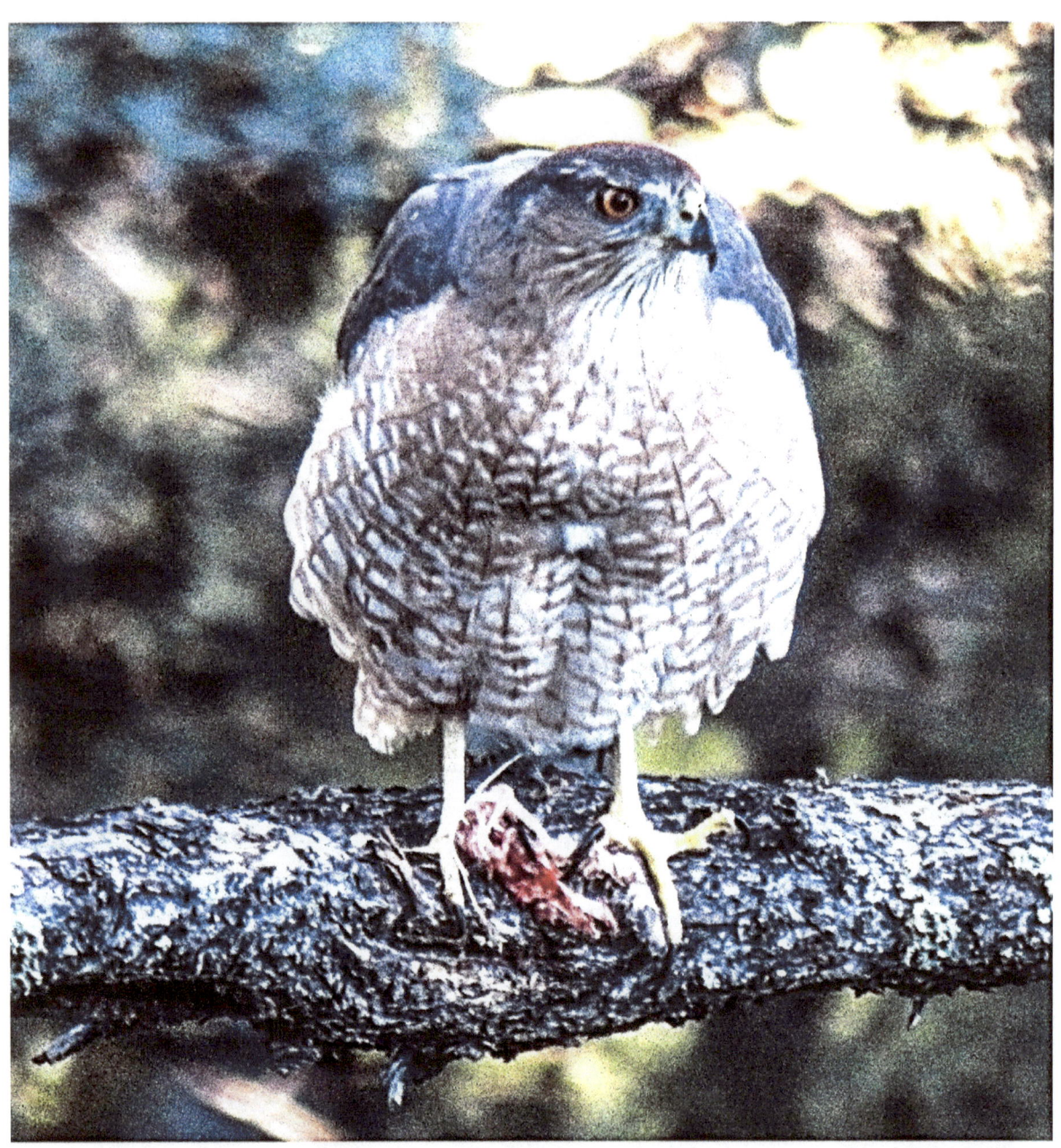

One last look at the Cooper's Hawk and its meal. Note in these pictures how there is a slight indentation between the thighs. Including this feather pattern will add a very realistic touch to your art.

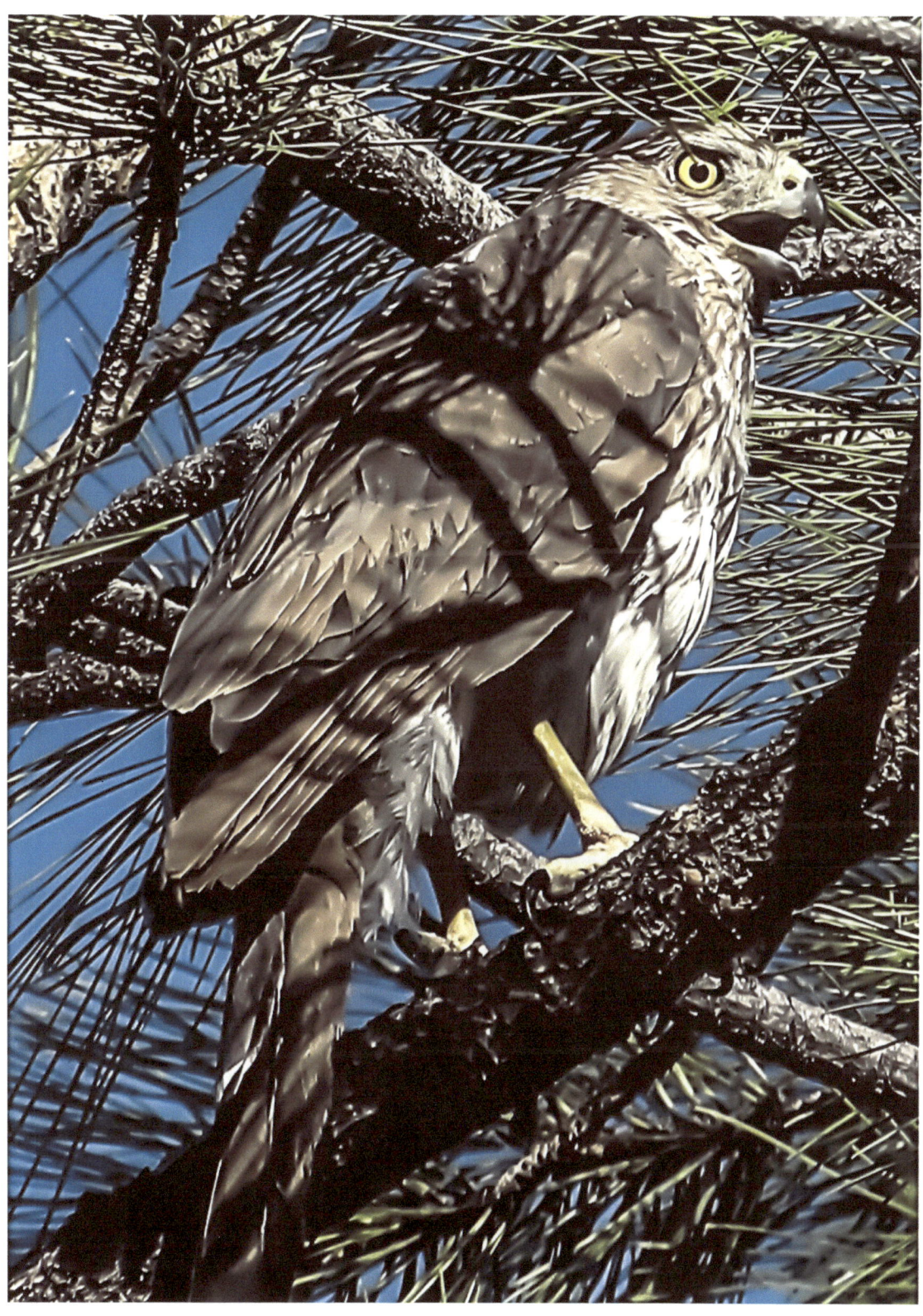

The coloration of a juvenile Cooper's Hawk helps camouflage it as it perches in a Ponderosa Pine awaiting a not too vigilant bird to fly by.

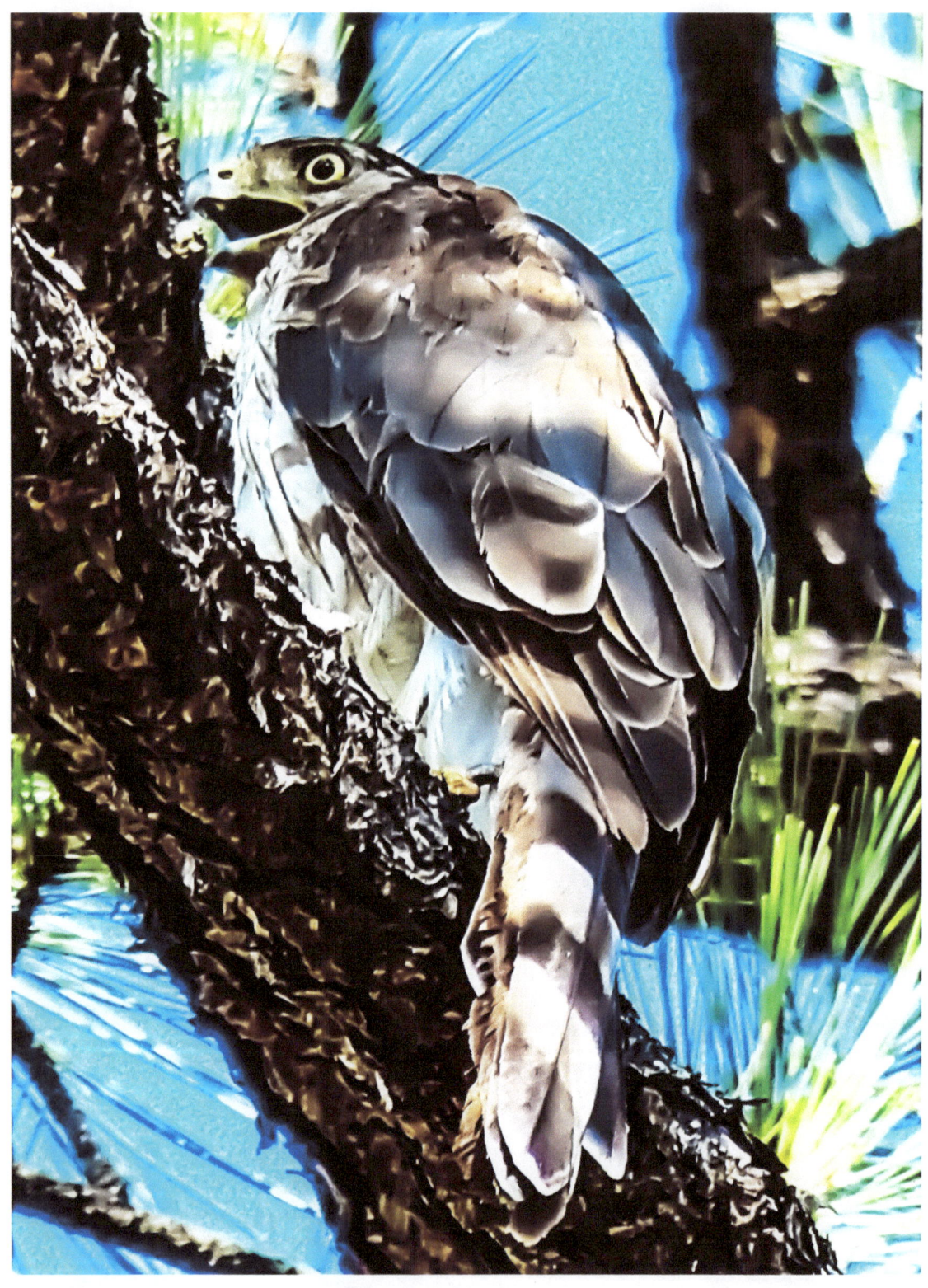

Cooper's Hawks usually build their nests 20 to 50 feet above the ground on a horizontal limb near the trunk. They can be very noisy and aggressive when defending a nest. This makes it very hard to get a picture of a nest.

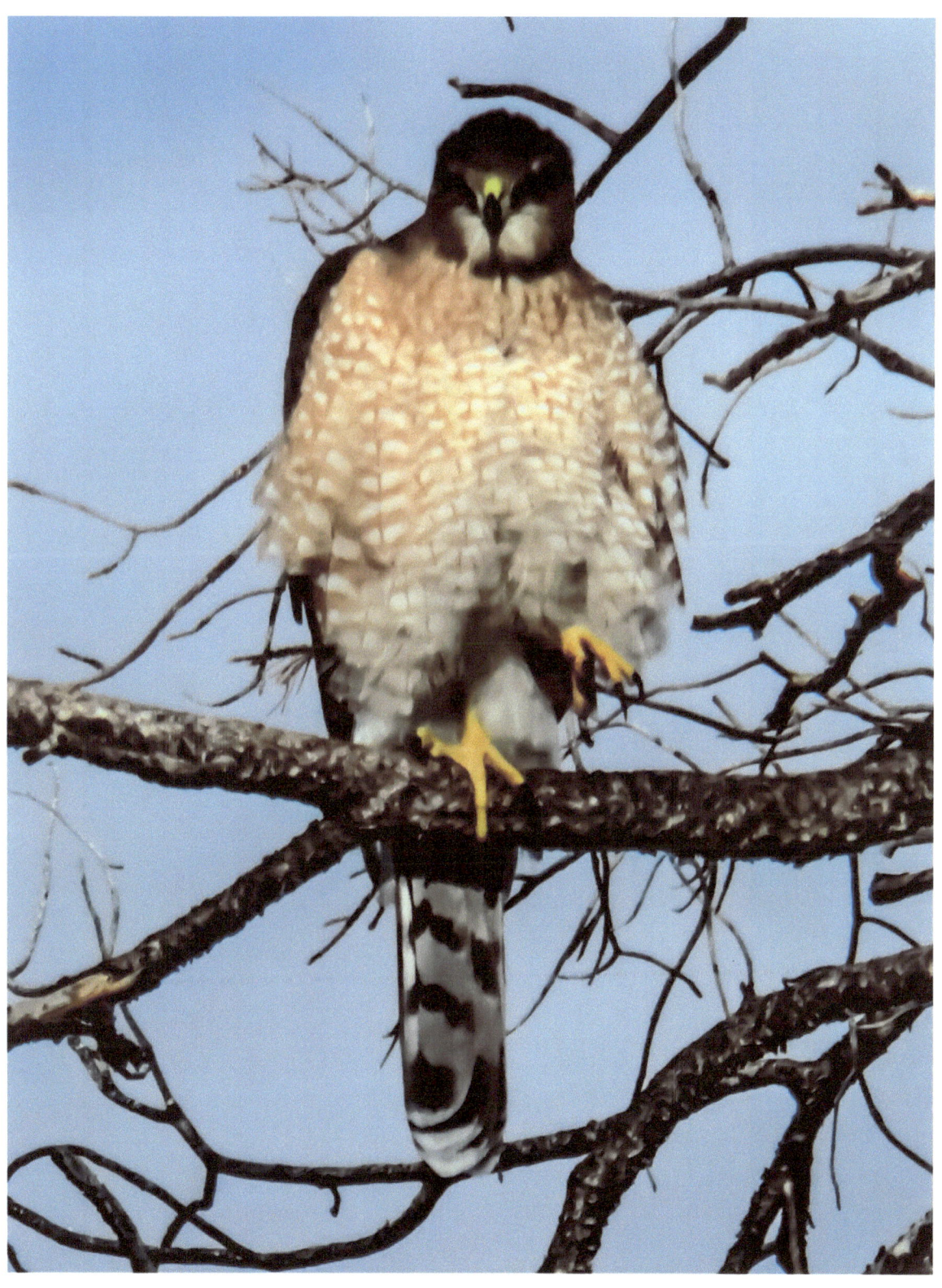

This picture is not of the best quality. It is included to show an unusual posture and tail pattern.

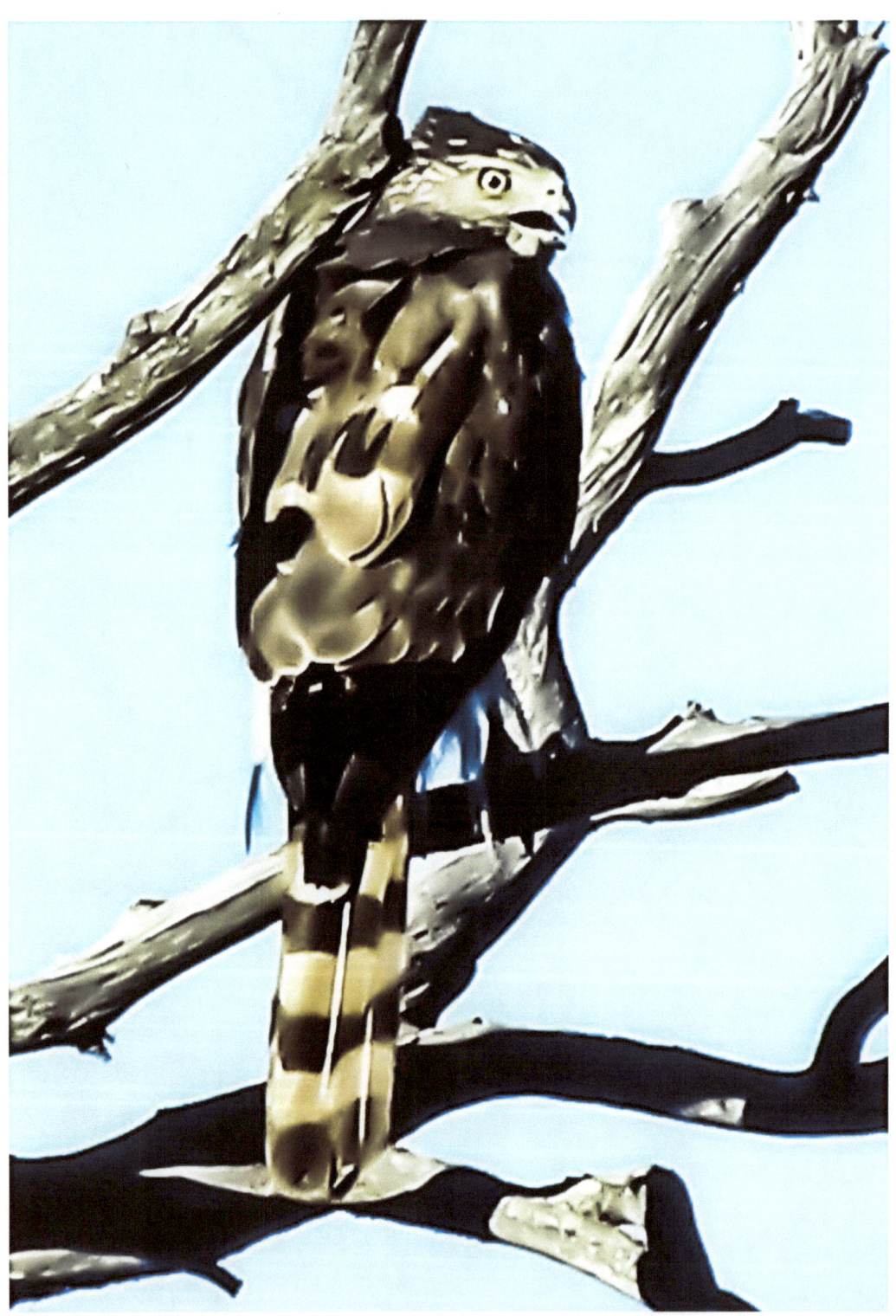

This is the same bird as on the next page. It is rather rare to get both the front and back of the same bird in consecutive pictures. It was moving around quite a bit because it was unhappy with me standing where I was.

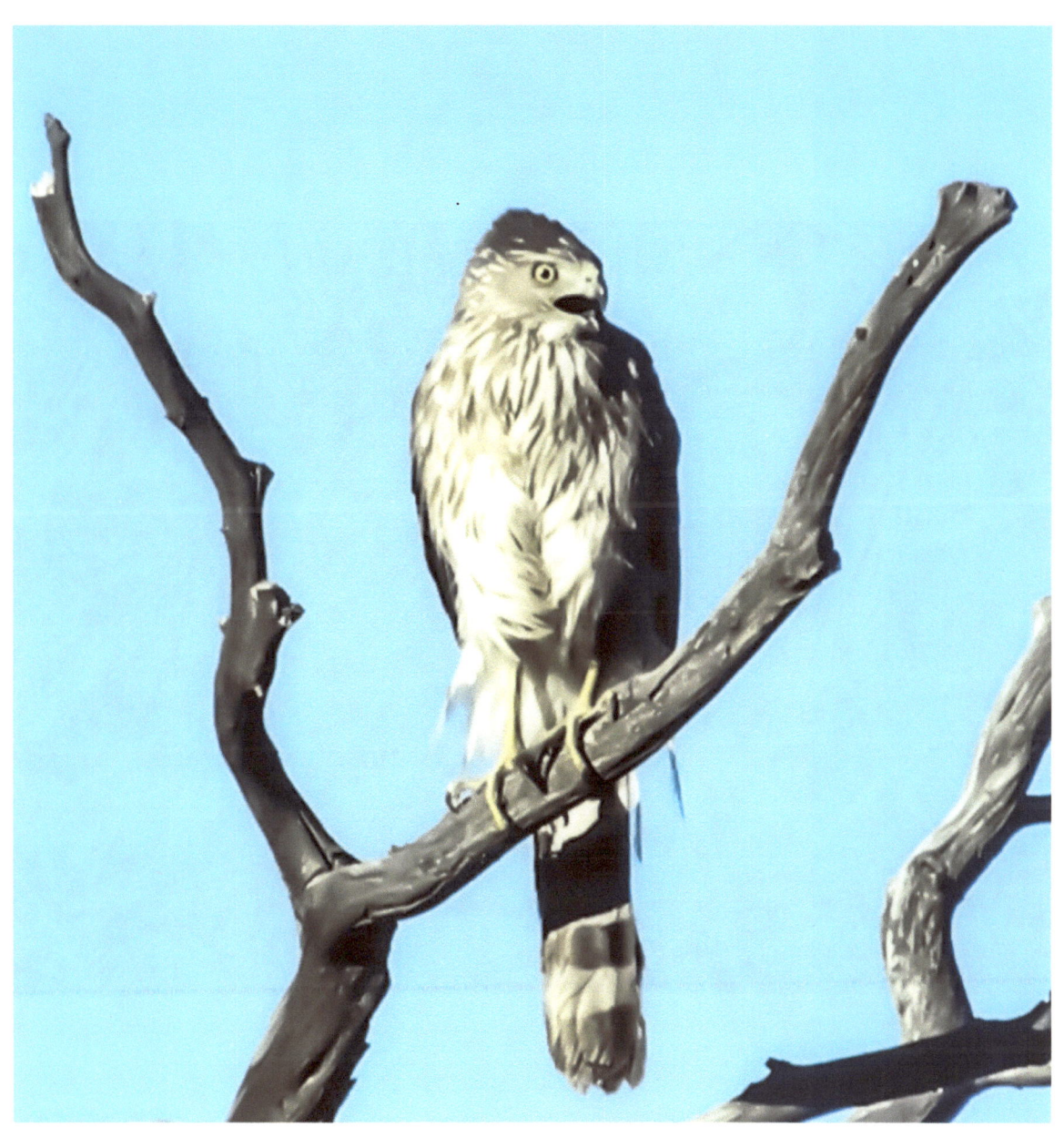

Various parts of a bird's body develop at different rates just as humans do. This bird shows the head shape, and tail pattern of an adult Cooper's Hawk. However, its eyes are still a juvenile yellow and its breast looks juvenile.

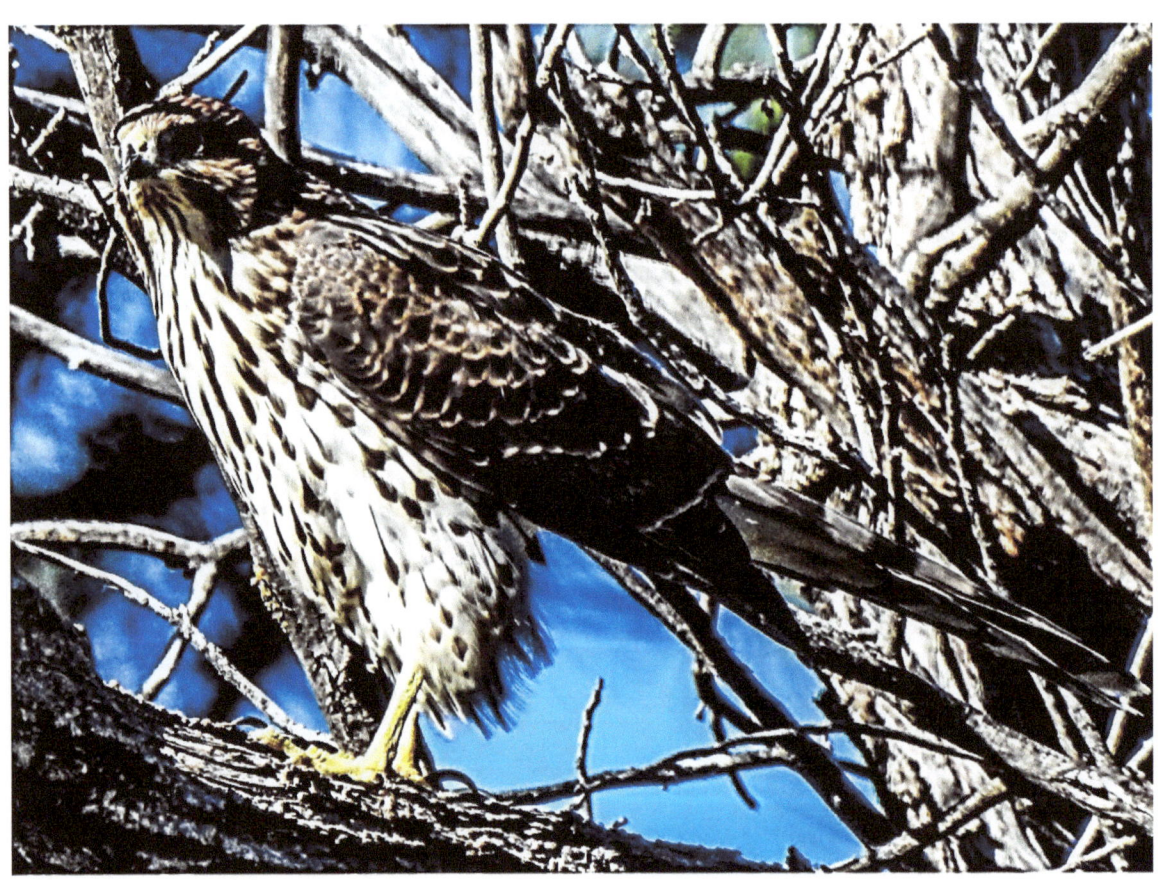

This is another illustration of how the plumage of a Cooper's Hawk helps it blend into its habitat. This is very important for being able to wait undetected to ambush prey.

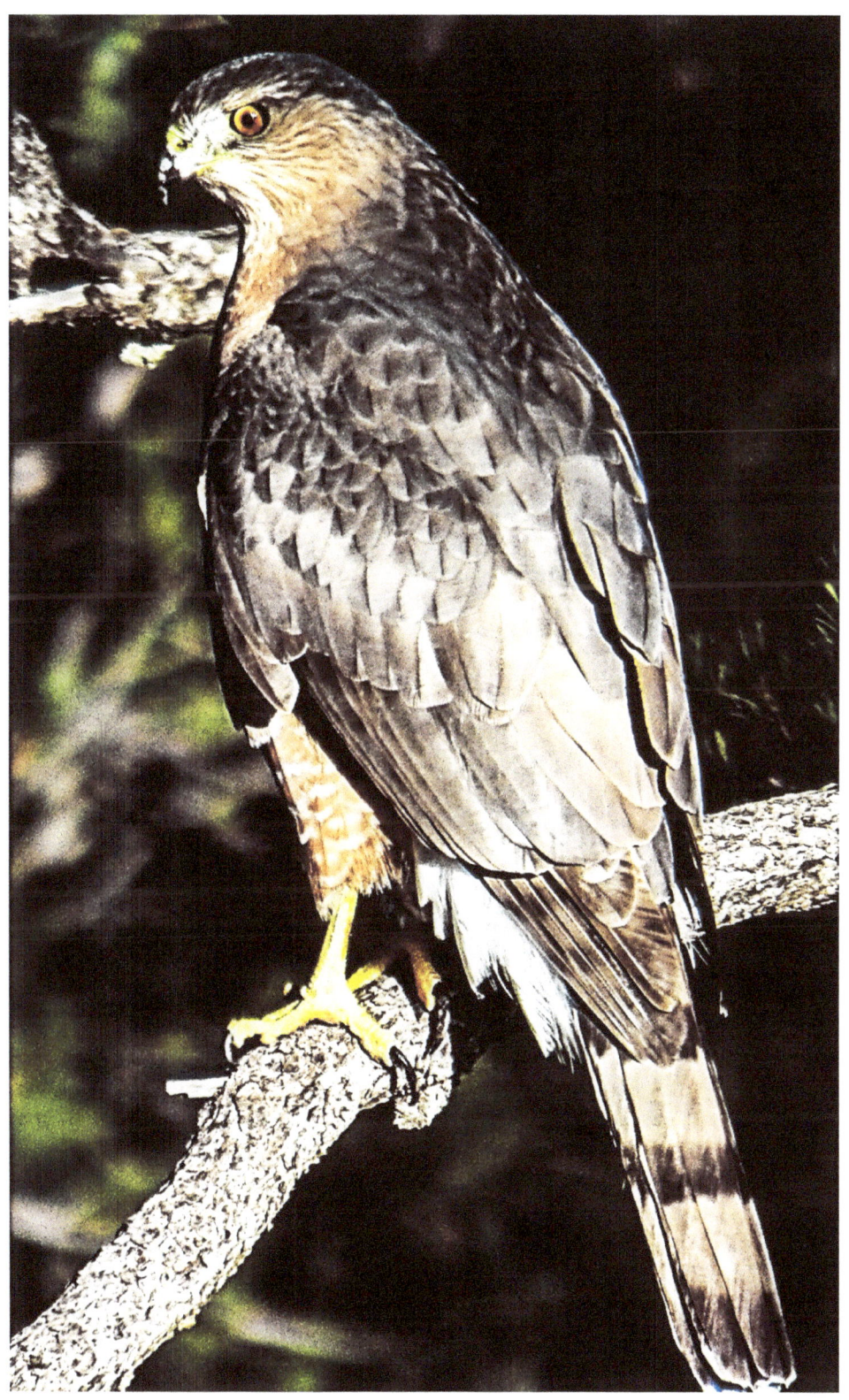

Cooper's Hawks are skillful fliers. I stepped out of my garage right into the path on one that was in full pursuit of a bird. It maneuvered past me through a narrow gap and continued on to catch its prey.

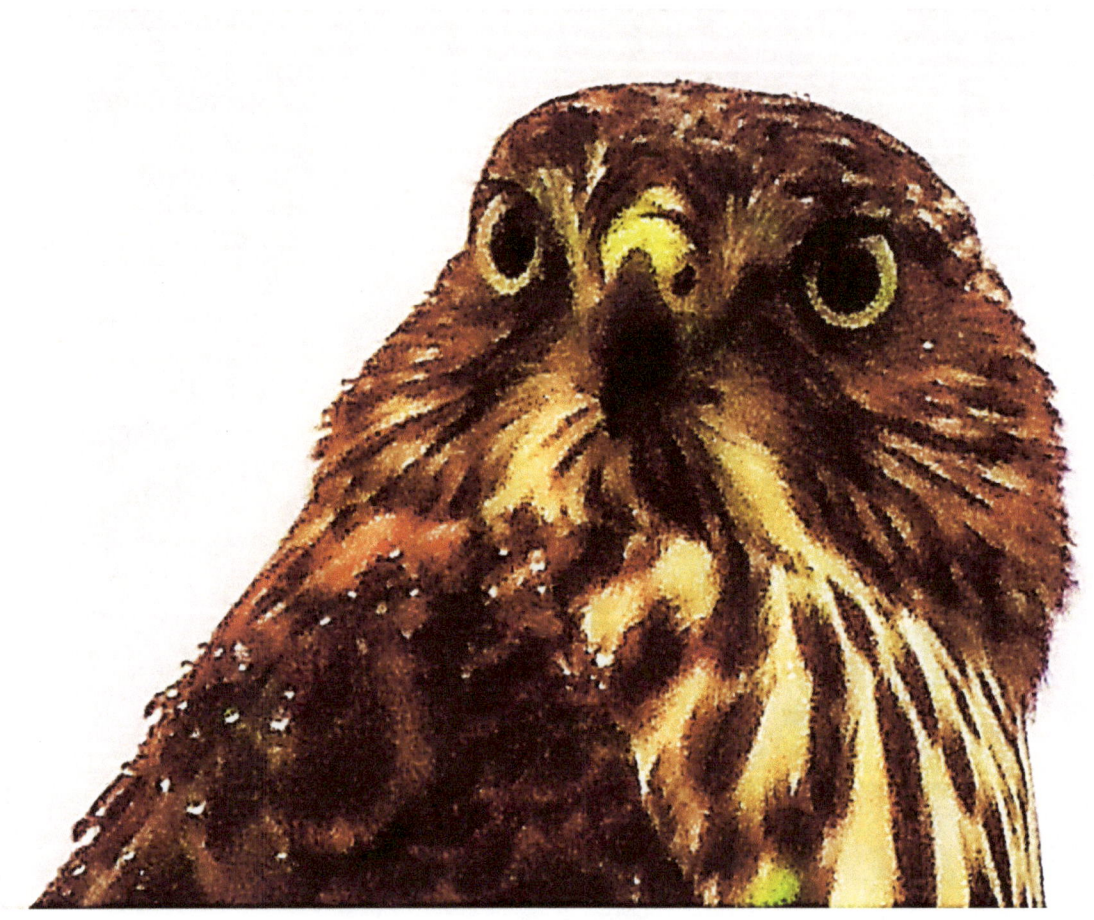

This juvenile Cooper's Hawk was sitting right outside my window in a downpour. Note the water droplets on its feathers.

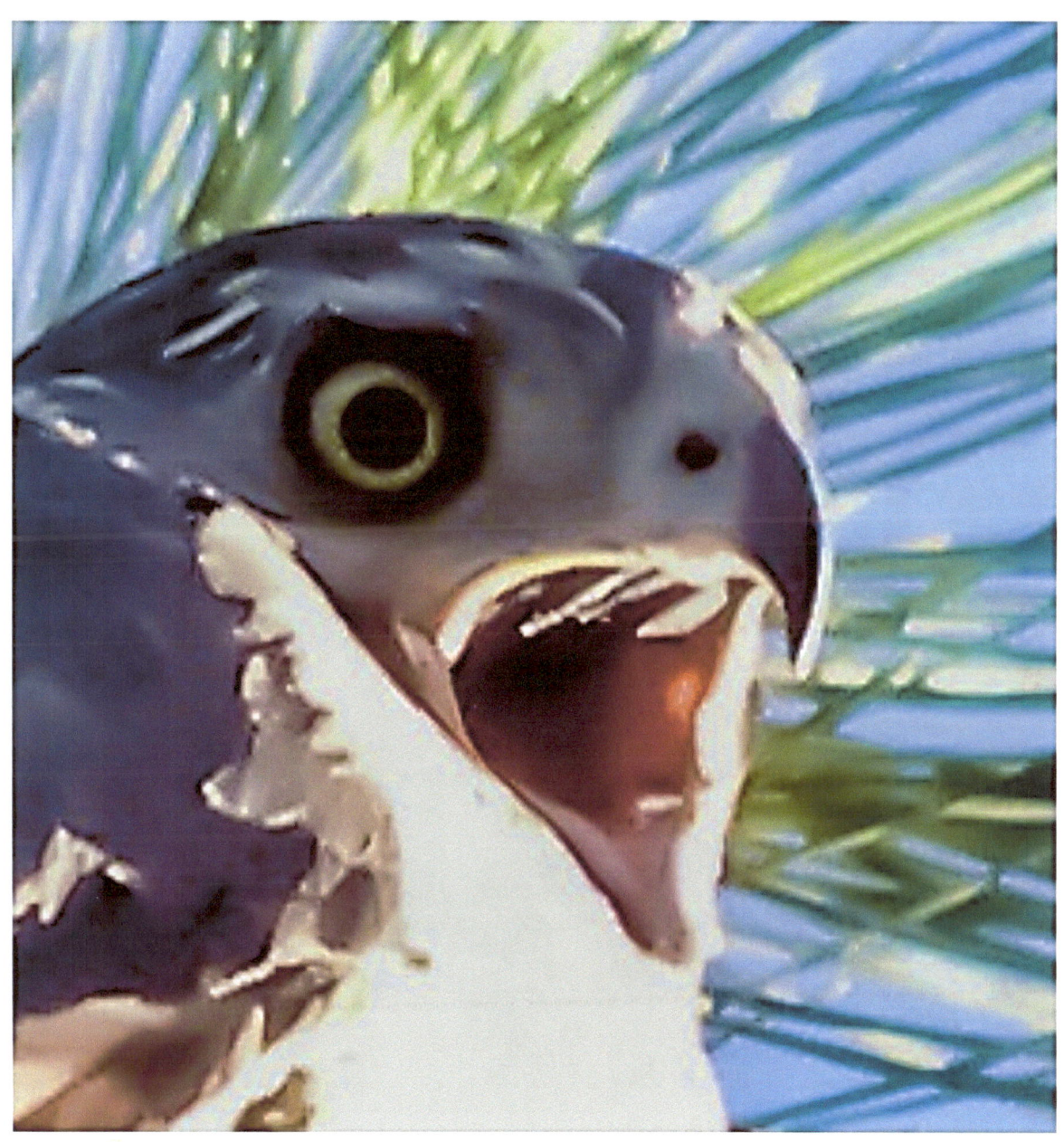

Note the almost tooth-like structures inside the mouth of a Cooper's Hawk that I photographed with a long telephoto lens. I have never seen another picture depicting these.

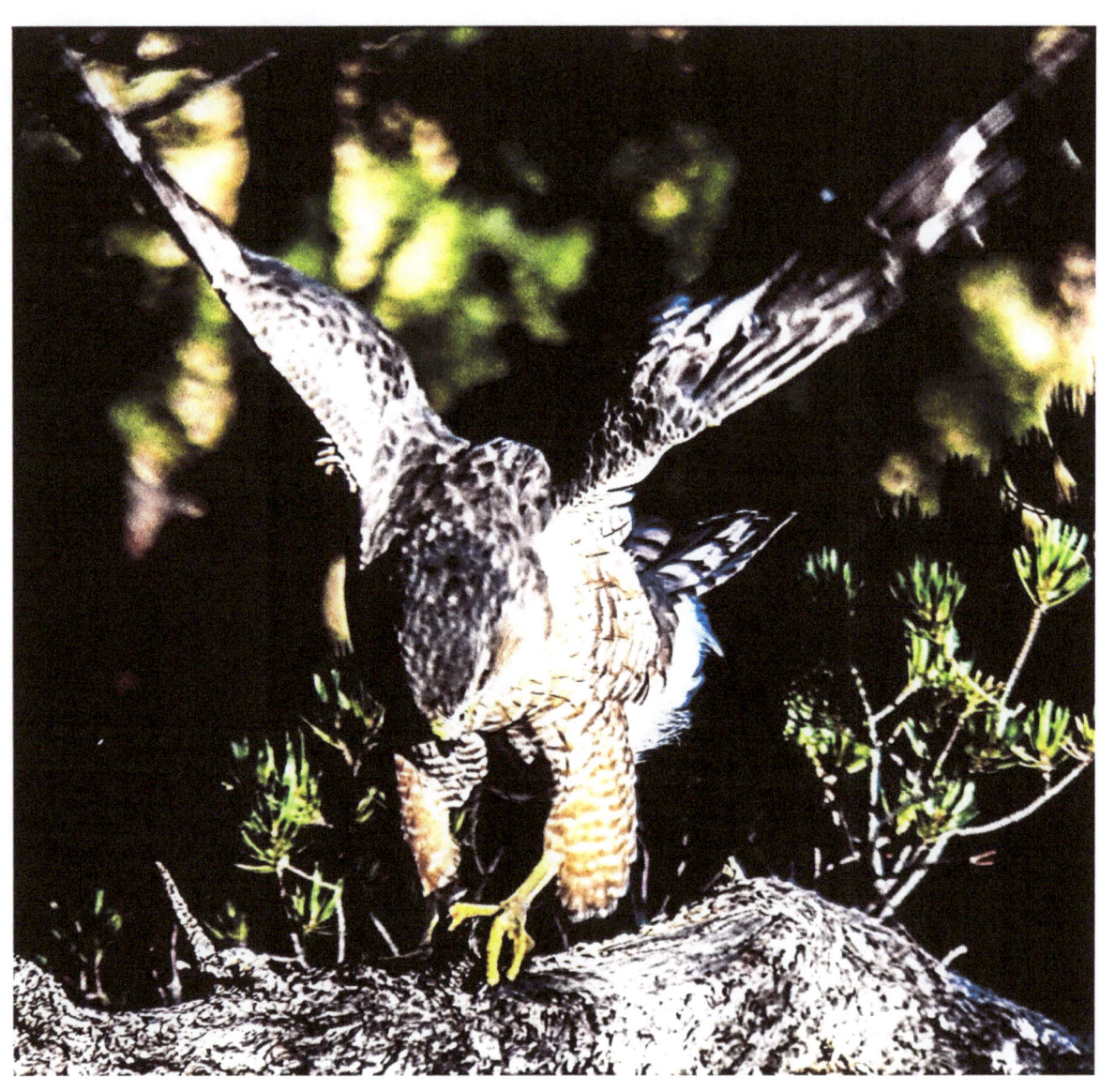

Enjoy your artistry. Good-bye.